We the People: It Begins with You!

Kelly Moyer

Published by Spirit & Soil Books, 2022.

Table of Contents

C ontents

KELLY MOYER

Published by **Spirit & Soil Books** Temecula, CA, 92591, USA

This revised edition includes updated material and additional Content.

_For more information, visit: www.kellysherbalblessings.com[1] or www.illuminatingselfgrowth.com[2]

---

1.   http://www.kellysherbalblessings.com1/

2.   http://www.illuminatingselfgrowth.com2/

Introduction

Thank you so much for choosing to read this book.

We the People: It Begins with You came to me in a dream—an inspired message meant to be shared. It is short, simple, and deeply heartfelt. I wrote this for those of us who feel called to be part of the solution, but may not know where or how to begin. Every action—big or small—can shine a light into the world. And we must be that light.

As I look around, I see a world that is both aching and awakening. Though we are all part of the same human family, we've become increasingly divided—separated by beliefs, labels, and fear. I see blame, pain, judgment, and confusion. I see people turning against one another and forgetting that our truest purpose is to love, support, and uplift each other.

But I also believe this is a powerful moment in time—a turning point not just for one country, but for the whole world. We cannot wait to be rescued. This is a collective calling. *We the People* are the answer. We are the ones we've been waiting for.

To bring the world back into balance, we must first return to love—starting with our connection to God, to each other, and to ourselves. Through unity, compassion, and personal responsibility, we rise. We must *live* our values daily. We must not just speak of change—we must embody it.

I wrote this book because I've witnessed too much division, too much fear, and too much silence. People have lost jobs, relationships, and freedoms for expressing their truth. Families have turned against each other. Censorship has taken root where open dialogue once lived. And too often, our rights and our humanity are being stripped away quietly, while we're distracted or discouraged.

This is not about politics. This is about *people*. This is about how far we've drifted from God, from truth, and from each other.

It is not okay to manipulate, silence, or cancel others based on differing beliefs or agendas. That is abuse, and we must name it as such.

But we can stand up for what's right without adding more anger and fear to the world. We can rise with love, with clarity, and with courage.

That's why I wrote this book—to offer a peaceful yet powerful path forward. A path of unity, of awareness, and of action. A path where each of us steps into our role, takes responsibility for our thoughts and behaviors, and joins hands with others to co-create a world where all can thrive.

WE WERE BORN FOR THIS time. And we are not powerless. We are *We the People*. We are *One*.

Let us rise together, with faith in God and love in our hearts. The world we dream of begins with us.

Our Constitution at a glance

I want to begin this section by saying—I am not a constitutional expert. Like many of you, I learned about the Constitution of the United States back in school, but didn't truly grasp the weight of its meaning until much later in life. It wasn't until I started doing my own research and digging deeper into its content that I realized just how important this foundational document truly is—and how much of it we may be taking for granted.

The one truth I have always held close is that we are born free.

Each of us has the right to think, speak, believe, and live according to our own inner truth. We are sovereign beings, and that freedom of choice is sacred. The Constitution exists to protect that right for every citizen.

That's why I've chosen to include a copy of the U.S. Constitution in the back of this book—because I believe it's time we remember what it actually says, what it stands for, and what it was created to do.

At its core, the Constitution was designed to protect the natural rights of the people and to build a unified government based on justice, peace, freedom, and the well-being of its citizens. It's not a relic of the past—it's a living guide, one that is meant to hold power in *our* hands: *We the People.*

But lately, it seems we're drifting further from that vision. I say this not with judgment, but with concern. I see many of our basic freedoms being questioned, challenged, or quietly overlooked. I see a growing divide among people, a disconnect from truth, and a sense that the voices of everyday citizens are being drowned out. This section of the book is a gentle reminder—of what is ours, what has been fought for, and what we must now protect.

You don't need to be a political expert to care about your freedoms. You just need to be willing to read, reflect, and reconnect with what this document represents. I've also included a link to a printable PDF version of the Constitution for your own study and reference. I encourage you to read it with fresh eyes and an open heart. It may stir something within you—an awakening to just how much we've accepted, and how much we still have the power to change.

Because knowledge is power. And *We the People* are far more powerful than we realize.

It Begins with You

Everything begins with you.

Your thoughts. Your words. Your actions. They all matter—more than you might realize.

Whether you're on a journey of spiritual growth or creating something meaningful in the world, every step you take has a ripple effect. We are all deeply connected, and what you choose to embody in your own life inevitably touches the lives of others. That's why it's so important that we take full responsibility for ourselves—our choices, our energy, and our healing.

I believe with all my heart that everything is energy. Everything is vibration. And when you raise your own energetic frequency—through love, awareness, and alignment—you help elevate the collective vibration of humanity. By healing and growing yourself, you become a beacon for others to do the same.

But it all starts within.

You cannot truly help others or make lasting change in the world without first taking care of yourself. Self-care is not selfish—it is foundational. It creates the strength, clarity, and compassion needed to serve and uplift others.

So how do we begin?

We begin by putting God first in our lives. By nurturing a personal relationship with the Divine, we anchor ourselves in truth and purpose. We learn to love ourselves—not in ego, but in wholeness. And from that sacred self-love, we naturally extend love to our neighbor. These are not abstract ideas. They are practices—daily choices that shape the way we live, relate, and serve.

In this book, I will share simple, intentional ways you can begin bringing these practices into your life. You don't need to follow every method—just find what resonates with you and let it grow from there. This is not about perfection. This is about progress, presence, and alignment.

As you commit to improving yourself, you may notice old stresses begin to fade. You may find more peace in your mind, more energy in your body, and more harmony in your relationships. Healing brings balance. And balance brings clarity.

Remember, this is a journey—and every small step matters. Let's begin with the most important one:

Putting God first.

I hope you find these practices nourishing and inspiring as you walk your own path of transformation.

God First

As I look at the growing division in our country and around the world, it's clear to me that many have turned away from God. In some areas of society, God is even being intentionally removed—from schools, communities, and conversations. But the truth is, we need God now more than ever.

God isn't someone to visit only on Sundays. God is meant to be with us in every moment, guiding our thoughts, words, and actions. God is always first.

Let me gently remind you—life is not just about *you*. Life is about God, the Creator of all things.

God is the everything and the everyone. We are all connected through the One, and that divine presence is within each of us. God is not somewhere far away—God is everywhere, all the time. And it's time for us to come back home to that truth.

It's time to return to love. It's time to live the teachings of Jesus—the Son of God—who showed us how to walk in love, compassion, humility, and truth. He didn't pick and choose who he helped based on their beliefs. He loved and served all. And so must we.

I encourage each and every one of us to build a personal relationship with God. We are the light of God in this world, and now is the time to rise and reflect that light more brightly than ever.

In this section, I'll share a few simple ways to put God first in your daily life—practices that have helped me connect more deeply with the Divine. When we put God first, not only are our own lives lifted, but we help raise the light in others as well. Faith builds strength. And the more of us who live in this light, the brighter the world becomes.

3 Ways to Keep God at the Center of Your Life

1. Prayer

PRAYER IS ONE OF THE most powerful ways to connect with God. And there is *no wrong way* to pray. You don't need fancy words or rituals—just an open heart and the willingness to be present with the Divine.

I begin each day by speaking with God before I even get out of bed. I thank Him for another day of life, I ask for guidance, and I send love to anyone who may need it. At night, I do the same. I release any stress or energy from the day, ask questions, express gratitude, seek forgiveness if needed, and again send love to others.

Your prayer practice will be unique to you. The most important thing is to make space for it every day. Talk to God often. Listen deeply. God hears you—always.

2. Meditation

MEDITATION ALLOWS US to quiet the noise and hear the still, small voice of God within us. It brings us into presence and helps us reconnect with our soul.

I meditate twice a day—once in the morning and again before bed. You can begin with just five minutes. Sit somewhere quiet, close your eyes, and focus on your breath. When your mind wanders, gently bring your attention back to your breathing. This is a simple form of mindful meditation, and it's a beautiful way to start.

There are many meditation styles, so find what feels right for you. The key is consistency. When we make time for stillness, we make room for God.

3. Serve Others

WE THE PEOPLE: IT BEGINS WITH YOU!

One of the most joyful ways to honor God is through service to others. When we lift others, we lift ourselves—and we lift the collective light of the world. God is in all of us, and serving others is a sacred act. There are endless ways to serve:

- Perform a random act of kindness
- Volunteer your time or skills
- Be present for someone who needs support
- Offer help when you see someone struggling
- Smile at a stranger—you never know the impact

Stay aware, stay kind, and stay open. Love is action, and service is love in motion.

Each of us has our own way of connecting with the God within. Find what works for you, and make it part of your daily life. When we put God first, we become better, stronger, and more compassionate people. We raise our vibration—and help raise the vibration of the world.

Let's return to what truly matters. Let's return to God. And let's rise—together, in His light.

Love Yourself

Learning to love yourself unconditionally is one of the most powerful and transformative things you can do. It sounds simple—and at its core, it is—but it requires intentional inner work. True self-love is a journey of returning home to who you really are. And it's essential.

You cannot fully love others until you learn to love yourself. When you cultivate deep compassion for yourself, it naturally overflows into your relationships, your community, and the world around you.

Below are three foundational ways to begin practicing self-love. Let these be starting points—guides to help you reconnect with your own worth, your needs, and your light.

1. Self-Care

TAKE GOOD CARE OF *you.*

We've all neglected ourselves at one time or another. Life gets busy—between jobs, family responsibilities, relationships, and household tasks, we often put our own care last on the list. But without intentional self-care, burnout, imbalance, and emotional exhaustion are never far behind.

Self-care isn't just about spa days or pampering (although those are wonderful too). True self-care is about honoring your needs, setting healthy boundaries, and making space for your well-being—mind, body, and spirit.

It can be as simple as creating a morning routine just for you, or learning to say "no" when your plate is already full. It can also mean saying "yes" when help is offered, without guilt or shame. Self-care is not selfish—it's foundational.

WE THE PEOPLE: IT BEGINS WITH YOU!

When you take care of yourself, you are more grounded, more energized, and more capable of showing up fully for others—without resentment or depletion.

Here are a few simple self-care ideas to inspire you:

- Journal with a cup of tea or coffee
- Take a mindful walk in nature
- Enjoy a cozy nap
- Read a book that feeds your soul
- Treat yourself to a facial (or give yourself one at home)
- Take a relaxing Epsom salt and lavender bath
- Get a massage or use self-massage techniques
- Light some candles and just *be*
- Garden, paint, create
- Watch a comforting or inspiring movie

The key is to find what nurtures you—and to *make it a habit*. Your well-being matters.

❧

1. Forgive Yourself

FORGIVENESS IS A POWERFUL act of self-love. Many of us carry guilt, shame, or regret—punishing ourselves for past choices, mistakes, or things we cannot change. But you deserve to be free. You deserve compassion.

Loving yourself means releasing judgment and embracing your humanity. You are not your past. You are so much more than the stories you've believed.

There are many tools and practices to support the process of forgiveness. Here are just a few to try:

- **Write a letter** to someone you need to forgive—or to yourself.

You don't have to send it. You can keep it, burn it, or tear it up. The healing is in the release.

- **Journal** your thoughts, feelings, and truths you've never had space to express.

- **Try Ho'oponopono**, a powerful Hawaiian practice of healing and forgiveness. It's simple and deeply effective. You can find many guides online to begin using this technique.

These practices help you clear emotional and energetic space—both consciously and subconsciously—so you can begin living with more peace, lightness, and freedom.

1. Know and Love Who You Are

TO TRULY LOVE YOURSELF, you must first *know* yourself. Spend time with yourself. Reflect. Explore. Connect with the truth of who you are, beyond roles, titles, and expectations.
   You might start by:

- Journaling about your passions, values, or dreams
- Trying something new that excites you
- Creating a **vision board** of who you are becoming
- Making a list of your positive traits, strengths, and unique gifts
- Spending quiet time in solitude and reflection
- Asking yourself: *What do I truly need right now? What brings me joy?*

This kind of self-exploration is healing. It deepens your relationship with *you*. And as your self-awareness grows, so will your confidence, your clarity, and your capacity to give and receive love.

WE THE PEOPLE: IT BEGINS WITH YOU!

Self-love is not a destination—it's a practice. It unfolds over time, in moments of awareness, gentleness, and truth. Make space for it. Prioritize it. And remember, as you love yourself more deeply, you will help raise the light in others too.

Because the more you love yourself, the more you live in alignment with the divine light within you. You are worthy. You are enough. And you are deeply loved.

Love Your Neighbor

L earn to love your neighbor unconditionally.
Many people will not associate with this person or that person based on the differences in beliefs or other differences.

We are surely a diverse world full of many types of people.

We are here to love our neighbor. By neighbor I do mean all of our brothers and sisters. So many are so busy running around with our own lives we don't slow down enough to notice our neighbor.

A few ways to begin showing our love is to first for ourselves, slow down. This way we may even notice our brothers and sisters. This can help us become aware of not just ourselves but of others.

You can also help someone that you may see struggling or just a kind gesture of opening the door for someone can lift a persons day. Random acts of kindness are also fun.

Lifting others up instead of putting them down can change the day. Not only this but when we lift others and then they lift others and when you lift others everyone's world becomes much brighter. Our entire world is lifted.

You can smile at a stranger. This raises your energetic vibration and it does theirs as well.

There are many ways but the ones that stand out the most are in acts of love and not through fear.

We are here to love each other and that includes all of our crazy differences. We each have the right to be exactly who we are and to freely speak our minds in love and not fear.

Take this love out into the world with you every minute of your life. Allow others to believe what they believe. Allow others to have their own opinions even when they do not match yours. Do this with love. Live in the higher vibration of life.

United We Stand

A Vision for Unity

My heart sees what is possible when we come together in unity. We are a beautifully diverse tapestry of people, each with unique experiences, perspectives, and gifts. And yet, at our core, we are one. One humanity. One shared home. One collective heart.

It will take *all* of us to create and sustain communities that are not only loving and supportive but truly thriving. No longer can we sit back and expect a few to carry the weight for many. The time has come for each of us to rise, take part, and contribute in our own meaningful way.

Working together—across differences, across beliefs, across borders—is how we will build a better world. Unity doesn't mean sameness. It means celebrating diversity while honoring our shared purpose. It means creating space for inclusion, where every voice matters and every heart is valued.

There are countless ways to begin. It doesn't require grand gestures. Sometimes, it starts with something as simple as donating clothing, offering a listening ear, or showing up for someone in need. Sometimes, it means engaging more deeply with your local community—participating in events, supporting grassroots efforts, or simply connecting with your neighbors.

In the following sections, I'll share ways you can begin to step into action—how we can all work together to co-create a more compassionate, connected, and conscious world.

Because *United, We Stand.*

And together, we can build something truly beautiful.

Community Involvement

Let's begin with something that truly has the power to uplift and transform: community involvement.

There are so many ways to make a difference right in your own neighborhood. It doesn't have to be overwhelming or time-consuming—even the smallest actions can ripple out in powerful ways. But it does take *all of us*. Now is the time to stop sitting back and waiting for change to happen. It's time to take a stand, show up, and get involved.

There's a place for everyone in this movement toward stronger, more loving communities. And the more of us who participate, the better life becomes for all.

Here are just a few ways you can become more involved in your community:

1. Volunteer Your Time

A) Hospitals

Many hospitals offer volunteer programs that support patients and staff. You might crochet baby hats or blankets, visit patients who are alone, or help with simple administrative tasks. Check your local hospital's website or give them a call to learn about opportunities.

B) Libraries

Libraries are always looking for volunteers! You could help re-shelve books, assist with events, or even read to children during story time.

C) Food Pantries

Your local food pantry often needs help unpacking donations, distributing food, or delivering items to families. Most pantries list opportunities online, or you can call them directly.

D) Hospice Care

Volunteering with hospice can be deeply meaningful. Whether you visit patients, bring a therapy pet, offer music or energy healing, or simply sit in companionship, you are making a difference.

E) Schools

You don't need to have children to volunteer at a school. Teachers often welcome help with grading, organizing, classroom assistance, or donations of supplies.

2. Attend Board Meetings

A) A) City Council Meetings

Stay informed and have your voice heard by attending your local government meetings. These meetings are a great way to learn what's happening in your city and take part in shaping your community.

B) School Board Meetings

If education is close to your heart, school board meetings are the perfect place to advocate for students and educators and understand what's being implemented in your school district.

c) HOA or PTA Meetings

Whether it's through your Homeowners' Association or Parent-Teacher Association, these gatherings give you a chance to build community and contribute ideas where you live or your children learn.

3. Start or Join a Group

Find a group aligned with your interests—or create one! Whether it's a walking group, a crafting circle, a faith-based fellowship, or a human rights advocacy group, connecting with others around a shared purpose strengthens your community.

4. Find a Church or Spiritual Group

Faith-based communities are a wonderful way to meet others and give back. Many churches offer outreach programs, volunteer days, and community events open to all.

5. Attend Local Events

Farmer's markets, festivals, fundraisers, and community gatherings bring neighbors together. They're a great way to support local initiatives and enjoy the beauty of community spirit.

⬥

6. Shop Local

Support small businesses, local artisans, and nearby farmers. When we shop locally, we uplift our neighbors—and often receive better, more meaningful products and services in return.

7. Take a Class

Enrich your life and meet new people by taking a class offered in your area. From painting and pottery to yoga, gardening, or cooking, there are countless ways to expand your skills and make new connections.

⬥

8. Donate Time, Services, or Goods
9.

GIVING DOESN'T ALWAYS mean money. Donate gently used clothing, offer your skills to a neighbor, help the elderly with groceries or errands, or do small acts of kindness like mowing a lawn or leaving a thoughtful note. Every action matters.

Community involvement is about connection, compassion, and contribution. It allows us to know our neighbors, offer our unique gifts, and co-create environments that are supportive, safe, and strong.

The more you look around, the more opportunities you'll find. This list is just the beginning

.

Together, we rise. And together, we create the world we want to live in.

Together We Can

Find your people. Seek out the groups, communities, and kindred spirits who share your heart for healing, love, and change. When we gather in unity—rooted in compassion and guided by purpose—we radiate a light that reaches far beyond our individual lives.

Share that love freely. Let it ripple outward. When our brothers and sisters come together with open hearts, united in love for all, we amplify the healing energy needed across the entire planet. Every act of connection, every moment of shared intention, adds to the collective vibration of hope and harmony.

It is more important now than ever before that we come together—not in sameness, but in shared humanity. Unity is not about agreement. It's about respect. It's about valuing each person's path, even when it looks different from our own. We don't need to think alike to stand together.

Each of us has a unique role to play on this earth. Your purpose is just as sacred as mine, and mine as yours. When we honor one another's gifts—even those we don't fully understand—we create a space where miracles can unfold. That's how communities are built. That's how healing takes root.

Together, we can rise above fear, beyond judgment, and into true connection.

Together, we can remember what it means to be *one people, under God,* walking side by side in love. The time is now. The power is within us.

And the beauty is—we don't have to do it alone.

Politics and our Involvement

Well I am going to try my best in this section. I have not been a particularly political person throughout my life. I have served more in a volunteer manor within our communities but on the politics end of things I really have not been too involved. I had to do much research in this area and I am just experiencing some of this myself. I will say that each and every one of us should learn what we can do to better our country and our communities. We have to work together. It takes all of us to rise up to the occasion.

I will share in this chapter what I have learned and what I am experiencing so far. Hopefully this can help everyone.

We are the people and we are the ones to make sure that our electors are doing their job for the people and not for their own agenda. When we do not stay aware we can become the victims of our society and not the solution.

We the people are in charge. When our government takes more than the people have given and we allow it we are no longer free.

One thing I want to say is just voting is not enough when it comes to keeping our electors accountable. We need to become the voices in our communities, in our states, and in our countries. We need to pay attention to what is happening all around us. We need to stay informed, collect the facts, and do the research to make sure what we think is happening is the truth.

There are many areas that we can look at to be a part of positive change. Some of these have grown way out of control and may need an overhaul. We do not need to stand back and do nothing.

Some areas that we may want to look at might be:

1. Is our voting system reliable or is it corrupt?
2. What is our Education system teaching our children?
3. How are our state and our local governments being run?
4. Immigration and the border issues?
5. Human rights issues.
6. Should we pay as much in taxes as we do and where does our money go (city, state and federal)?
7. Homeless solutions. (mental health, addiction, or affordable living)
8. Bills being passed through legislature that the people might not ever see or hear about.
9. What is our United States government doing for us or against we the people?
10. Are our freedoms being stomped on somewhere?

These are only a few examples of things you can look at and there may be much more happening behind the scenes as you dig into an area you may have a concern with.

Many of us don't even know where to begin when we see these things happening so we just block it out as if we think we have no control over any of it.

Here I will post a few ideas of things that can make a world of difference when we are trying to improve our communities.

A good place to begin is at the local and state level and there are many ways to go about this.

I have had much luck recently reaching out to our State representative. I wrote her a letter of my concerns and I have attended some of her Town Hall meetings. You can find your representatives on your states websites and their contact info as well. You can call, email, write letters, or visit meetings if they hold them. You can also look up other government officials on the state government site and all of the contact info is usually included there as well.

If you want to get more involved in human rights issues you may find non-government organizations or non-profits that address a specific area that you would like to address.

Also for elections you can get more involved by volunteering.

As far as bills that get passed or not through the legislature you can do some lobbying for or against the bills which brings you closer to working with your electors. Also Interest groups are groups of individuals organized around a specific interest or issue that band together in order to advocate for certain policy measures. These groups are often very focused in what they are trying to accomplish so it would really depend on what important interests or concerns you have that would decide what interest group would be the best to get involved with.

For Education you would want to go to your school board meetings. In some cases this makes a big difference. If not come together with other parents to build better solutions. You can come together and create groups to get ideas on how to resolve your issue.

FOR MORE COUNTY ISSUES you may want to go to a county board meeting or even for your city a city board meeting. These are great ways to see what is happening in your community and to stand up if needed. You can write letters, call, or email these officials as well.

You can write letters to your local paper, serve on task forces, email elected representatives or provide input on proposed new policies.

You can start your own group or non-profit or even your own organization. You can organize a peaceful protest. A big lesson here is to be an informed citizen and stand up with your community to resolve these issues together.

We will all have different opinions but overall we all also want what is best for each of us. It takes many differences together to build one successful community. One where we all keep our GOD given freedoms.

Stand up for Your Rights with Love

Freedom, Respect, and the Power of Love
We may not all agree on every issue—and that's okay. But there is one truth we must all come to agree on: each of us is free to think, believe, and be who we are. That freedom is sacred.

We are not here to harm, bully, or silence one another. We are here to love our neighbors, to lift each other up, and to walk side by side—especially in our differences. It takes every one of us to build strong, thriving communities. Our diversity is not a weakness—it's a strength. And when we unite with open hearts and shared purpose, we can overcome any challenge and create solutions that benefit us all.

In the United States, we are blessed to have the Constitution and its Amendments—documents designed to protect the rights and freedoms of *every* citizen. These protections are not selective. They are for *all* of us. But rights not protected and practiced can slowly disappear. We must be vigilant. We must stay awake. And we must be willing to stand up for these freedoms—not just for ourselves, but for others too.

Not everyone will share your beliefs, and you won't share theirs. That's the nature of a free society. Some will stand with you; some will stand apart. That is their right, just as it is yours. What we cannot allow is for disagreement to become division, or difference to become dehumanization.

Name-calling, shaming, and violence are not acts of love. Cutting people out of your life simply because they see the world differently is not the way forward.

Hate and fear will never bring lasting change. They are not the answers—and they are certainly not aligned with God's truth.

There is a better way.

You can be bold and brave while still being kind. You can be assertive without attacking. You can stand firm in your truth and still hold space for someone else's. That is real strength. That is real love.

Sometimes, we must simply agree to disagree—and keep showing up as who we are anyway. With love. With grace. With faith.

Because in the end, it's not about always being right. It's about always choosing what is *righteous*.

Be the Solution

As we come to the end of this book, there are a few things I feel called to leave with you—truths from my heart that I hope will stir something within yours.

Too often, we sit quietly while the world shifts around us. Sometimes we see the problems clearly but feel powerless to change them, waiting for someone else to take the lead. Sometimes we grow weary and choose silence. Other times, we convince ourselves that the issues are too big, too complicated, or not ours to face.

But here's the truth:

- We are the ones we've been waiting for.
- You have the power to make a difference.
- Together, we have the power to transform everything.

Yes, the challenges we face are real—within our communities, our country, and around the world. Our education systems, government structures, healthcare models, food practices, and the growing crisis of homelessness are just a few of the areas crying out for attention and healing. And while the issues may be vast, the solution is still the same: **us.**

There is always room for improvement. Always space for change. And it is up to **We the People** to step forward, take ownership, and be

31

part of the rebuilding and re-imagining of a better world. A world that works for all.

But we cannot do this work without first returning to our Source. It all begins with **God**.

We must reconnect with Divine truth, align our hearts with love, and ground ourselves in faith. From that place of spiritual strength, we can do the inner work—healing, learning, growing—and then extend that work outward, into our families, neighborhoods, and communities.

This inner transformation is not a one-time event. It is a practice. A commitment. A journey.

Healing the world begins with healing ourselves and releasing fear, shame, and limitation. Reclaiming the sacred connection to our hearts, our purpose, and to one another. As we tend to our own soul soil, we become better stewards of the collective.

We must also remember that no act of love or service is ever too small.

Planting a seed of hope, showing up with kindness, speaking the truth when it's hard, these are all forms of light. You don't have to change the whole world. But you *can* change your corner of it. And that ripple matters more than you know.

So ask yourself:

- Where am I being called to show up more fully?
- What gifts do I carry that the world needs now?
- What does it look like to lead with compassion, even when it's hard?

There is wisdom in your lived experience. Power in your voice. Healing in your hands. And guidance within your spirit. You don't need to have it all figured out. You just need to be willing to begin.

Be brave enough to listen. Be bold enough to act. Be gentle enough to rest.

WE THE PEOPLE: IT BEGINS WITH YOU!

And be rooted enough in your faith that you never forget who walks with you. Let this be a beginning, not an end.

Let this be the moment where you decide to rise. To step into your power. To choose love over fear.

To walk hand-in-hand with others toward healing, justice, and peace.

Because united, we truly can stand. And together—we can rise.

The Constitution of the United States

1 "US Constitution." Cong. Rsch. Serv., Constitution of the United States: Analysis and Interpretation, https://constitution.congress.gov (last visited September 27, 2022)

The Preamble

We the People of the United States, in Order to form a more perfect Union, establish Justice, insure domestic Tranquility, provide for the common defense, promote the general Welfare, and secure the Blessings of Liberty to ourselves and our Posterity, do ordain and establish this Constitution for the United States of America.

Article I

Section 1: Congress

All legislative Powers herein granted shall be vested in a Congress of the United States, which shall consist of a Senate and House of Representatives.

Section 2: The House of Representatives

The House of Representatives shall be composed of Members chosen every second Year by the People of the several States, and the Electors in each State shall have the Qualifications requisite for Electors of the most numerous Branch of the State Legislature.

No Person shall be a Representative who shall not have attained to the Age of twenty five Years, and been seven Years a Citizen of the United States, and who shall not, when elected, be an Inhabitant of that State in which he shall be chosen. Representatives and direct Taxes shall be apportioned among the several States which may be included within this Union, according to their respective Numbers, which shall be determined by adding to the whole Number of free Persons, including those bound to Service for a Term of Years, and excluding Indians not taxed, three fifths of all other Persons. The actual Enumeration shall be made within three Years after the first Meeting of the Congress of the United States, and within every subsequent Term of ten Years, in such Manner as they shall by Law direct. The Number of Representatives shall not exceed one for every thirty Thousand, but each State shall have at Least one Representative; and until such enumeration shall be made, the

State of New Hampshire shall be entitled to chuse three, Massachusetts eight, Rhode-Island and Providence Plantations one, Connecticut five, New-York six, New Jersey four, Pennsylvania eight,

Delaware one, Maryland six, Virginia ten, North Carolina five, South Carolina five, and Georgia three.

When vacancies happen in the Representation from any State, the Executive Authority thereof shall issue Writs of Election to fill such Vacancies.

The House of Representatives shall chuse their Speaker and other Officers; and shall have the sole Power of Impeachment.

Section 3: The Senate

The Senate of the United States shall be composed of two Senators from each State, chosen by the Legislature thereof for six Years; and each Senator shall have one Vote.

Immediately after they shall be assembled in Consequence of the first Election, they shall be divided as equally as may be into three Classes. The Seats of the Senators of the first Class shall be vacated at the Expiration of the second Year, of the second Class at the Expiration of the fourth Year, and of the third Class at the Expiration of the sixth Year, so that one third may be chosen every second Year; and if Vacancies happen by Resignation, or otherwise, during the Recess of the Legislature of any State, the Executive thereof may make temporary Appointments until the next Meeting of the Legislature, which shall then fill such Vacancies.

No Person shall be a Senator who shall not have attained to the Age of thirty Years, and been nine Years a Citizen of the United States, and who shall not, when elected, be an Inhabitant of that State for which he shall be chosen.

The Vice President of the United States shall be President of the Senate, but shall have no Vote, unless they be equally divided.

WE THE PEOPLE: IT BEGINS WITH YOU!

The Senate shall chuse their other Officers, and also a President pro tempore, in the Absence of the Vice President, or when he shall exercise the Office of President of the United States.

The Senate shall have the sole Power to try all Impeachments. When sitting for that Purpose, they shall be on Oath or Affirmation. When the President of the United States is tried, the Chief Justice shall preside: And no Person shall be convicted without the Concurrence of two thirds of the Members present.

41

Judgment in Cases of Impeachment shall not extend further than to removal from Office, and disqualification to hold and enjoy any Office of honor, Trust or Profit under the United States: but the Party convicted shall nevertheless be liable and subject to Indictment, Trial, Judgment and Punishment, according to Law.

Section 4:

The Times, Places and Manner of holding Elections for Senators and Representatives, shall be prescribed in each State by the Legislature thereof; but the Congress may at any time by Law make or alter such Regulations, except as to the Places of chusing Senators.

The Congress shall assemble at least once in every Year, and such Meeting shall be on the first Monday in December, unless they shall by Law appoint a different Day.

Section 5:

Each House shall be the Judge of the Elections, Returns and Qualifications of its own Members, and a Majority of each shall constitute a Quorum to do Business; but a smaller Number may adjourn from day to day, and may be authorized to compel the Attendance of absent Members, in such Manner, and under such Penalties as each House may provide.

Each House may determine the Rules of its Proceedings, punish its Members for disorderly Behaviour, and, with the Concurrence of two thirds, expel a Member.

Each House shall keep a Journal of its Proceedings, and from time to time publish the same, excepting such Parts as may in their Judgment require Secrecy; and the Yeas and Nays of the Members of either House on any question shall, at the Desire of one fifth of those Present, be entered on the Journal.

Neither House, during the Session of Congress, shall, without the Consent of the other, adjourn for more than three days, nor to any other Place than that in which the two Houses shall be sitting.

Section 6:

The Senators and Representatives shall receive a Compensation for their Services, to be ascertained by Law, and paid out of the Treasury of the United States. They shall in all Cases, except Treason, Felony and Breach of the Peace, be privileged from Arrest during their Attendance at the Session of their respective Houses, and in going to and returning from the same; and for any Speech or Debate in either House, they shall not be questioned in any other Place.

No Senator or Representative shall, during the Time for which he was elected, be appointed to any civil Office under the Authority of the United States, which shall have been created, or the Emoluments whereof shall have been encreased during such time; and no Person holding any Office under the United States, shall be a Member of either House during his Continuance in Office.

Section 7:

All Bills for raising Revenue shall originate in the House of Representatives; but the Senate may propose or concur with Amendments as on other Bills.

Every Bill which shall have passed the House of Representatives and the Senate, shall, before it become a Law, be presented to the President of the United States: If he approve he shall sign it, but if not he shall return it, with his Objections to that House in which it shall have originated, who shall enter the Objections at large on their Journal, and proceed to reconsider it. If after such Reconsideration two thirds of that House shall agree to pass the Bill, it shall be sent, together with the Objections, to the other House, by which it shall likewise be reconsidered, and if approved by two thirds of that House, it shall become a Law. But in all such Cases the Votes of both Houses shall be determined by yeas and Nays, and the Names of the Persons voting for and against the Bill shall be entered on the Journal of each House respectively. If any Bill shall not be returned by the President within ten Days (Sundays excepted) after it shall have been presented to him, the Same shall be a Law, in like Manner as if he had signed it, unless the Congress by their Adjournment prevent its Return, in which Case it shall not be a Law.

Every Order, Resolution, or Vote to which the Concurrence of the Senate and House of Representatives may be necessary (except on a question of Adjournment) shall be presented to the President of the United States; and before the Same shall take Effect, shall be approved by him, or being disapproved by him, shall be repassed by two thirds of the Senate and House of Representatives, according to the Rules and Limitations prescribed in the Case of a Bill.

Section 8:

The Congress shall have Power To lay and collect Taxes, Duties, Imposts and Excises, to pay the Debts and provide for the common Defence and general Welfare of the United States; but all Duties, Imposts and Excises shall be uniform throughout the United States;

To borrow Money on the credit of the United States;

To regulate Commerce with foreign Nations, and among the several States, and with the Indian Tribes;

To establish an uniform Rule of Naturalization, and uniform Laws on the subject of Bankruptcies throughout the United States;

To coin Money, regulate the Value thereof, and of foreign Coin, and fix the Standard of Weights and Measures; To provide for the Punishment of counterfeiting the Securities and current Coin of the United States;

To establish Post Offices and post Roads;

To promote the Progress of Science and useful Arts, by securing for limited Times to Authors and Inventors the exclusive Right to their respective Writings and Discoveries;

To constitute Tribunals inferior to the supreme Court;

To define and punish Piracies and Felonies committed on the high Seas, and Offences against the Law of Nations; To declare War, grant Letters of Marque and Reprisal, and make Rules concerning Captures on Land and Water; To raise and support Armies, but no Appropriation

of Money to that Use shall be for a longer Term than two Years; To
provide and maintain a Navy; To make Rules for the Government and
Regulation of the land and naval Forces; To provide for calling forth
the Militia to execute the Laws of the Union, suppress Insurrections and
repel Invasions; To provide for organizing, arming, and disciplining, the
Militia, and for governing such Part of them as may be employed in
the Service of the United States, reserving to the States respectively, the
Appointment of the Officers, and the Authority of training the Militia
according to the discipline prescribed by Congress;

To exercise exclusive Legislation in all Cases whatsoever, over such
District (not exceeding ten Miles square) as may, by Cession of particular
States, and the Acceptance of Congress, become the Seat of the
Government of the United States, and to exercise like Authority over
all Places purchased by the Consent of the Legislature of the State in
which the Same shall be, for the Erection of Forts, Magazines, Arsenals,
dock-Yards, and other needful Buildings;–And To make all Laws which
shall be necessary and proper for carrying into Execution the foregoing
Powers, and all other Powers vested by this Constitution in the
Government of the United States, or in any Department or Officer
thereof.

Section 9:
The Migration or Importation of such Persons as any of the States
now existing shall think proper to admit, shall not be prohibited by the
Congress prior to the Year one thousand eight hundred and eight, but
a Tax or duty may be imposed on such Importation, not exceeding ten
dollars for each Person.

The Privilege of the Writ of Habeas Corpus shall not be suspended,
unless when in Cases of Rebellion or Invasion the public Safety may
require it.

No Bill of Attainder or ex post facto Law shall be passed.

No Capitation, or other direct, Tax shall be laid, unless in Proportion
to the Census or enumeration herein before directed to be taken.

No Tax or Duty shall be laid on Articles exported from any State.

No Preference shall be given by any Regulation of Commerce or Revenue to the Ports of one State over those of another; nor shall Vessels bound to, or from, one State, be obliged to enter, clear, or pay Duties in another.

No Money shall be drawn from the Treasury, but in Consequence of Appropriations made by Law; and a regular Statement and Account of the Receipts and Expenditures of all public Money shall be published from time to time.

No Title of Nobility shall be granted by the United States: And no Person holding any Office of Profit or Trust under them, shall, without the Consent of the Congress, accept of any present, Emolument, Office, or Title, of any kind whatever, from any King, Prince, or foreign State.

Section 10:

No State shall enter into any Treaty, Alliance, or Confederation; grant Letters of Marque and Reprisal; coin Money; emit Bills of Credit; make any Thing but gold and silver Coin a Tender in Payment of Debts; pass any Bill of Attainder, ex post facto Law, or Law impairing the Obligation of Contracts, or grant any Title of Nobility.

No State shall, without the Consent of the Congress, lay any Imposts or Duties on Imports or Exports, except what may be absolutely necessary for executing it's inspection Laws: and the net Produce of all Duties and Imposts, laid by any State on Imports or Exports, shall be for the Use of the Treasury of the United States; and all such Laws shall be subject to the Revision and Controul of the Congress.

No State shall, without the Consent of Congress, lay any Duty of Tonnage, keep Troops, or Ships of War in time of Peace, enter into any Agreement or Compact with another State, or with a foreign Power, or engage in War, unless actually invaded, or in such imminent Danger as will not admit of delay.

Article II

Section 1:

The executive Power shall be vested in a President of the United States of America. He shall hold his Office during the Term of four Years, and, together with the Vice President, chosen for the same Term, be elected, as follows:

Each State shall appoint, in such Manner as the Legislature thereof may direct, a Number of Electors, equal to the whole Number of Senators and Representatives to which the State may be entitled in the Congress: but no Senator or Representative, or Person holding an Office of Trust or Profit under the United States, shall be appointed an Elector.

The Electors shall meet in their respective States, and vote by Ballot for two Persons, of whom one at least shall not be an Inhabitant of the same State with themselves. And they shall make a List of all the Persons voted for, and of the Number of Votes for each; which List they shall sign and certify, and transmit sealed to the Seat of the Government of the United States, directed to the President of the Senate. The President of the Senate shall, in the Presence of the Senate and House of Representatives, open all the Certificates, and the Votes shall then be counted. The Person having the greatest Number of Votes shall be the President, if such Number be a Majority of the whole Number of Electors appointed; and if there be more than one who have such Majority, and have an equal Number of Votes, then the House of Representatives shall immediately chuse by Ballot one of them for President; and if no Person have a Majority, then from the five highest on the List the said House shall in like Manner chuse the President.

But in chusing the President, the Votes shall be taken by States, the Representation from each State having one Vote; A quorum for this purpose shall consist of a Member or Members from two thirds of the States, and a Majority of all the States shall be necessary to a Choice. In every Case, after the Choice of the President, the Person having the greatest Number of Votes of the Electors shall be the Vice President. But if there should remain two or more who have equal Votes, the Senate shall chuse from them by Ballot the Vice President.

The Congress may determine the Time of chusing the Electors, and the Day on which they shall give their Votes; which Day shall be the same throughout the United States.

No Person except a natural born Citizen, or a Citizen of the United States, at the time of the Adoption of this Constitution, shall be eligible to the Office of President; neither shall any Person be eligible to that Office who shall not have attained to the Age of thirty five Years, and been fourteen Years a Resident within the United States.

In Case of the Removal of the President from Office, or of his Death, Resignation, or Inability to discharge the Powers and Duties of the said Office, the Same shall devolve on the Vice President, and the Congress may by Law provide for the Case of Removal, Death, Resignation or Inability, both of the President and Vice President, declaring what Officer shall then act as President, and such Officer shall act accordingly, until the Disability be removed, or a President shall be elected.

The President shall, at stated Times, receive for his Services, a Compensation, which shall neither be increased nor diminished during the Period for which he shall have been elected, and he shall not receive within that Period any other Emolument from the United States, or any of them.

Before he enter on the Execution of his Office, he shall take the following Oath or Affirmation:–"I do solemnly swear (or affirm) that I will faithfully execute the Office of President of the United States, and will to the best of my Ability, preserve, protect and defend the Constitution of the United States."

Section 2:

The President shall be Commander in Chief of the Army and Navy of the United States, and of the Militia of the several States, when called into the actual Service of the United States; he may require the Opinion, in writing, of

the principal Officer in each of the executive Departments, upon any Subject relating to the Duties of their respective Offices, and he shall have Power to grant Reprieves and Pardons for Offences against the United States, except in Cases of Impeachment.

He shall have Power, by and with the Advice and Consent of the Senate, to make Treaties, provided two thirds of the Senators present concur; and he shall nominate, and by and with the Advice and Consent of the Senate, shall appoint Ambassadors, other public Ministers and Consuls, Judges of the supreme Court, and all other Officers of the United States, whose Appointments are not herein otherwise provided for, and which shall be established by Law: but the Congress may by Law vest the Appointment of such inferior Officers, as they think proper, in the President alone, in the Courts of Law, or in the Heads of Departments.

The President shall have Power to fill up all Vacancies that may happen during the Recess of the Senate, by granting Commissions which shall expire at the End of their next Session.

Section 3:

He shall from time to time give to the Congress Information of the State of the Union, and recommend to their Consideration such Measures as he shall judge necessary and expedient; he may, on extraordinary Occasions, convene both Houses, or either of them, and in Case of Disagreement between them, with Respect to the Time of Adjournment, he may adjourn them to such Time as he shall think proper; he shall receive Ambassadors and other public Ministers; he shall take Care that the Laws be faithfully executed, and shall Commission all the Officers of the United States.

Section 4:

The President, Vice President and all civil Officers of the United States, shall be removed from Office on Impeachment for, and Conviction of, Treason, Bribery, or other high Crimes and Misdemeanors.

Article III

Section 1:

The judicial Power of the United States shall be vested in one supreme Court, and in such inferior Courts as the Congress may from time to time ordain and establish. The Judges, both of the supreme and inferior Courts, shall hold their Offices during good Behaviour, and shall, at stated Times, receive for their Services a Compensation, which shall not be diminished during their Continuance in Office.

Section 2:

The judicial Power shall extend to all Cases, in Law and Equity, arising under this Constitution, the Laws of the United States, and Treaties made, or which shall be made, under their Authority;–to all Cases affecting Ambassadors, other public Ministers and Consuls;–to all Cases of admiralty and maritime Jurisdiction;–to Controversies to which the United States shall be a Party;–to Controversies between two or more States;– between a State and Citizens of another State,–between Citizens of different States,–between Citizens of the same State claiming Lands under Grants of different States, and between a State, or the Citizens thereof, and foreign States, Citizens or Subjects.

In all Cases affecting Ambassadors, other public Ministers and Consuls, and those in which a State shall be Party, the supreme Court shall have original Jurisdiction. In all the other Cases before mentioned, the supreme Court shall have appellate Jurisdiction, both as to Law and Fact, with such Exceptions, and under such Regulations as the Congress shall make.

The Trial of all Crimes, except in Cases of Impeachment, shall be by Jury; and such Trial shall be held in the State where the said Crimes shall have been committed; but when not committed within any State, the Trial shall be at such Place or Places as the Congress may by Law have directed.

Section 3:

Treason against the United States, shall consist only in levying War against them, or in adhering to their Enemies, giving them Aid and Comfort. No Person shall be convicted of Treason unless on the Testimony of two Witnesses to the same overt Act, or on Confession in open Court.

The Congress shall have Power to declare the Punishment of Treason, but no Attainder of Treason shall work Corruption of Blood, or Forfeiture except during the Life of the Person attainted.

Article IV

S ection 1:

S   Full Faith and Credit shall be given in each State to the public Acts, Records, and judicial Proceedings of every other State. And the Congress may by general Laws prescribe the Manner in which such Acts, Records and Proceedings shall be proved, and the Effect thereof.

Section 2:

The Citizens of each State shall be entitled to all Privileges and Immunities of Citizens in the several States.

A Person charged in any State with Treason, Felony, or other Crime, who shall flee from Justice, and be found in another State, shall on Demand of the executive Authority of the State from which he fled, be delivered up, to be removed to the State having Jurisdiction of the Crime.

No Person held to Service or Labour in one State, under the Laws thereof, escaping into another, shall, in Consequence of any Law or Regulation therein, be discharged from such Service or Labour, but shall be delivered up on Claim of the Party to whom such Service or Labour may be due.

Section 3:

New States may be admitted by the Congress into this Union; but no new State shall be formed or erected within the Jurisdiction of any other State; nor any State be formed by the Junction of two or more States, or Parts of States, without the Consent of the Legislatures of the States concerned as well as of the Congress.

The Congress shall have Power to dispose of and make all needful Rules and Regulations respecting the Territory or other Property belonging to the United States; and nothing in this Constitution shall be so construed as to Prejudice any Claims of the United States, or of any particular State.

Section 4:

The United States shall guarantee to every State in this Union a Republican Form of Government, and shall protect each of them against Invasion; and on Application of the Legislature, or of the Executive (when the Legislature cannot be convened), against domestic Violence.

Article V

The Congress, whenever two thirds of both Houses shall deem it necessary, shall propose Amendments to this Constitution, or, on the Application of the Legislatures of two thirds of the several States, shall call a Convention for proposing Amendments, which, in either Case, shall be valid to all Intents and Purposes, as Part of this Constitution, when ratified by the Legislatures of three fourths of the several States, or by Conventions in three fourths thereof, as the one or the other Mode of Ratification may be proposed by the Congress; Provided that no Amendment which may be made prior to the Year One thousand eight hundred and eight shall in any Manner affect the first and fourth Clauses in the Ninth Section of the first Article; and that no State, without its Consent, shall be deprived of its equal Suffrage in the Senate.

Article VI

All Debts contracted and Engagements entered into, before the Adoption of this Constitution, shall be as valid against the United States under this Constitution, as under the Confederation.

This Constitution, and the Laws of the United States which shall be made in Pursuance thereof; and all Treaties made, or which shall be made, under the Authority of the United States, shall be the supreme Law of the Land; and the Judges in every State shall be bound thereby, any Thing in the Constitution or Laws of any State to the Contrary notwithstanding. The Senators and Representatives before mentioned, and the Members of the several State Legislatures, and all executive and judicial Officers, both of the United States and of the several States, shall be bound by Oath or Affirmation, to support this Constitution; but no religious Test shall ever be required as a Qualification to any Office or public Trust under the United States.

Article VII

The Ratification of the Conventions of nine States, shall be sufficient for the Establishment of this Constitution between the States so ratifying the Same.

Done in Convention, by the unanimous consent of the States present, the seventeenth day September, in the year of our Lord one thousand seven hundred and eighty-seven, and of the independence of the United States of America the twelfth. In witness whereof we have hereunto subscribed our names.

Attest William Jackson Secretary

Go: Washington -Presidt. and deputy from Virginia

Delaware

GEO: READ
 Gunning Bedford jun John Dickinson Richard Bassett
 Jaco: Broom

Virginia

JOHN BLAIR—
 James Madison Jr.

WE THE PEOPLE: IT BEGINS WITH YOU!

South Carolina

J. RUTLEDGE
    Charles Cotesworth Pinckney
    Charles Pinckney
    Pierce Butler.

New Hampshire

John Langdon Nicholas Gilman

Connecticut

Wm. Saml. Johnson Roger Sherman

New Jersey

Wil. Livingston David Brearley. Wm. Paterson. Jona: Dayton

Maryland

JAMES MCHENRY
    Dan of St Thos. Jenifer Danl Carroll.

North Carolina

WM BLOUNT
    Richd. Dobbs Spaight.
    Hu Williamson

Georgia

WILLIAM FEW

Abr Baldwin

Massachusetts

Nathaniel Gorham Rufus King

New York

Alexander Hamilton

Pennsylvania

B FRANKLIN
Thomas Mifflin Robt Morris Geo. Clymer Thos. FitzSimons Jared Ingersoll
James Wilson. Gouv Morris

Bill of Rights

The Bill of Rights are amendments to the articles in the Constitution. I have listed them below.

Amendments to the Constitution

First Amendment

CONGRESS SHALL MAKE no law respecting an establishment of religion, or prohibiting the free exercise thereof; or abridging the freedom of speech, or of the press; or the right of the people peaceably to assemble, and to petition the Government for a redress of grievances.

Second Amendment

A WELL REGULATED MILITIA, being necessary to the security of a free State, the right of the people to keep and bear Arms, shall not be infringed.

Third Amendment

NO SOLDIER SHALL, IN time of peace be quartered in any house, without the consent of the Owner, nor in time of war, but in a manner to be prescribed by law.

Fourth Amendment

THE RIGHT OF THE PEOPLE to be secure in their persons, houses, papers, and effects, against unreasonable searches and seizures, shall not be violated, and no Warrants shall issue, but upon probable cause, supported by Oath or affirmation, and particularly describing the place to be searched, and the persons or things to be seized.

Fifth Amendment

NO PERSON SHALL BE held to answer for a capital, or otherwise infamous crime, unless on a presentment or indictment of a Grand Jury, except in cases arising in the land or naval forces, or in the Militia, when in actual service in time of War or public danger; nor shall any person be subject for the same offence to be twice put in jeopardy of life or limb; nor shall be compelled in any criminal case to be a witness against himself, nor be deprived of life, liberty, or property, without due process of law; nor shall private property be taken for public use, without just compensation.

Sixth Amendment

IN ALL CRIMINAL PROSECUTIONS, the accused shall enjoy the right to a speedy and public trial, by an impartial jury of the State and district wherein the crime shall have been committed, which district shall have been previously ascertained by law, and to be informed of the nature and cause of the accusation; to be confronted with the witnesses against him; to have compulsory process for obtaining witnesses in his favor, and to have the Assistance of Counsel for his defence.

Seventh Amendment

IN SUITS AT COMMON law, where the value in controversy shall exceed twenty dollars, the right of trial by jury shall be preserved, and no fact tried by a jury, shall be otherwise re-examined in any Court of the United States, than according to the rules of the common law.

Eighth Amendment

EXCESSIVE BAIL SHALL not be required, nor excessive fines imposed, nor cruel and unusual punishments inflicted.

Ninth Amendment

THE ENUMERATION IN the Constitution, of certain rights, shall not be construed to deny or disparage others retained by the people.

Tenth Amendment

THE POWERS NOT DELEGATED to the United States by the Constitution, nor prohibited by it to the States, are reserved to the States respectively, or to the people.

Attest,

John Beckley, Clerk of the House of Representatives. Sam. A. Otis Secretary of the Senate.

Frederick Augustus Muhlenberg Speaker of the House of Representatives. John Adams, Vice-President of the United States, and President of the Senate. (end of the Bill of Rights)

Eleventh Amendment

THE JUDICIAL POWER of the United States shall not be construed to extend to any suit in law or equity, commenced or prosecuted against one of the United States by Citizens of another State, or by Citizens or Subjects of any Foreign State.

Twelfth Amendment

THE ELECTORS SHALL meet in their respective states, and vote by ballot for President and Vice-President, one of whom, at least, shall not be an inhabitant of the same state with themselves; they shall name in their ballots the person voted for as President, and in distinct ballots the person voted for as Vice-President, and they shall make distinct lists of all persons voted for as President, and of all persons voted for as Vice-President, and of the number of votes for each, which lists they shall sign and certify, and transmit sealed to the seat of the government of the United States, directed to the President of the Senate;—The President of the Senate shall, in the presence of the Senate and House of Representatives, open all the certificates and the votes shall then be counted;—The person having the greatest number of votes for President, shall be the President, if such number be a majority of the whole number of Electors appointed; and if no person have such majority, then from the persons having the highest numbers not exceeding three on the list of those voted for as President, the House of Representatives shall choose immediately, by ballot, the President. But in choosing the President, the votes shall be taken by states, the representation from each state having one vote; a quorum for this purpose shall consist of a member or members from two-thirds of the states, and a majority of all the states shall be necessary to a choice. And if the House of Representatives shall not choose a President whenever the right of choice shall devolve upon them, before the fourth day of March next following, then the

Vice-President shall act as President, as in the case of the death or other constitutional disability of the President. note 14[1] —The person having the greatest number of votes as Vice-President, shall be the Vice-President, if such number be a majority of the whole number of Electors appointed, and if no person have a majority, then from the two highest numbers on the list, the Senate shall choose the Vice-President; a quorum for the purpose shall consist of two-thirds of the whole number of Senators, and a majority of the whole number shall be necessary to a choice. But no person constitutionally ineligible to the office of President shall be eligible to that of Vice-President of the United States.

Thirteenth Amendment

NEITHER SLAVERY NOR involuntary servitude, except as a punishment for crime whereof the party shall have been duly convicted, shall exist within the United States, or any place subject to their jurisdiction.

Congress shall have power to enforce this article by appropriate legislation.

Fourteenth Amendment

1: ALL PERSONS BORN or naturalized in the United States, and subject to the jurisdiction thereof, are citizens of the United States and of the State wherein they reside. No State shall make or enforce any law which shall abridge the privileges or immunities of citizens of the United States; nor shall any State deprive any person of life, liberty, or property, without due process of law; nor deny to any person within its jurisdiction the equal protection of the laws.

2: Representatives shall be apportioned among the several States according to their respective numbers, counting the whole number of persons in each State, excluding Indians not taxed. But when the right to vote at any election for the choice of electors for President and Vice President of the United States, Representatives in Congress, the Executive and Judicial officers of a State, or the members of the Legislature thereof, is denied to any of the male inhabitants of such State, being twenty-one years of age, and citizens of the United States, or in any way abridged, except for participation in rebellion, or other crime, the basis of representation therein shall be reduced in the proportion which the number of such male citizens shall bear to the whole number of male citizens twenty-one years of age in such State.

3: No person shall be a Senator or Representative in Congress, or elector of President and Vice President, or hold any office, civil or military, under the United States, or under any State, who, having previously taken an oath, as a member of Congress, or as an officer of the United States, or as a member of any State legislature, or as an executive or judicial officer of any State, to support the Constitution of the United States, shall have engaged in insurrection or rebellion against the same, or given aid or comfort to the enemies thereof. But Congress may by a vote of two-thirds of each House, remove such disability.

4: The validity of the public debt of the United States, authorized by law, including debts incurred for payment of pensions and bounties for services in suppressing insurrection or rebellion, shall not be questioned. But neither the United States nor any State shall assume or pay any debt or obligation incurred in aid of insurrection or rebellion against the United States, or any claim for the loss or emancipation of any slave; but all such debts, obligations and claims shall be held illegal and void.

5: The Congress shall have power to enforce, by appropriate legislation, the provisions of this article.

Fifteenth Amendment

The right of citizens of the United States to vote shall not be denied or abridged by the United States or by any State on account of race, color, or previous condition of servitude.

The Congress shall have power to enforce this article by appropriate legislation.

Sixteenth Amendment

THE CONGRESS SHALL have power to lay and collect taxes on incomes, from whatever source derived, without apportionment among the several States, and without regard to any census or enumeration.

Seventeenth Amendment

1: THE SENATE OF THE United States shall be composed of two Senators from each State, elected by the people thereof, for six years; and each Senator shall have one vote. The electors in each State shall have the qualifications requisite for electors of the most numerous branch of the State legislatures.

2: When vacancies happen in the representation of any State in the Senate, the executive authority of such State shall issue writs of election to fill such vacancies: Provided, That the legislature of any State may empower the executive thereof to make temporary appointments until the people fill the vacancies by election as the legislature may direct.

3: This amendment shall not be so construed as to affect the election or term of any Senator chosen before it becomes valid as part of the Constitution..

Eighteenth Amendment

1: AFTER ONE YEAR FROM the ratification of this article the manufacture, sale, or transportation of intoxicating liquors within, the importation thereof into, or the exportation thereof from the United States and all territory subject to the jurisdiction thereof for beverage purposes is hereby prohibited.

2: The Congress and the several States shall have concurrent power to enforce this article by appropriate legislation.

3: This article shall be inoperative unless it shall have been ratified as an amendment to the Constitution by thelegislatures of the several States, as provided in the Constitution, within seven years from the date of the submission hereof to the States by the Congress.

***

Nineteenth Amendment

THE RIGHT OF CITIZENS of the United States to vote shall not be denied or abridged by the United States or by any State on account of sex.

Congress shall have power to enforce this article by appropriate legislation.

Twentieth Amendment

1: THE TERMS OF THE President and Vice President shall end at noon on the 20th day of January, and the terms of Senators and Representatives at noon on the 3d day of January, of the years in which such terms would have ended if this article had not been ratified; and the terms of their successors shall then begin.

2: The Congress shall assemble at least once in every year, and such meeting shall begin at noon on the 3d day of January, unless they shall by law appoint a different day.

3: If, at the time fixed for the beginning of the term of the President, the President elect shall have died, the Vice President elect shall become President. If a President shall not have been chosen before the time fixed for the beginning of his term, or if the President elect shall have failed to qualify, then the Vice President elect shall act as President until a

President shall have qualified; and the Congress may by law provide for the case wherein neither a President elect nor a Vice President elect shall have qualified, declaring who shall then act as President, or the manner in which one who is to act shall be selected, and such person shall act accordingly until a President or Vice President shall have qualified.

4: The Congress may by law provide for the case of the death of any of the persons from whom the House of Representatives may choose a President whenever the right of choice shall have devolved upon them, and for the case of the death of any of the persons from whom the Senate may choose a Vice President whenever the right of choice shall have devolved upon them.

5: Sections 1 and 2 shall take effect on the 15th day of October following the ratification of this article.

6: This article shall be inoperative unless it shall have been ratified as an amendment to the Constitution by the legislatures of three-fourths of the several States within seven years from the date of its submission.

Twenty-First Amendment

1: THE EIGHTEENTH ARTICLE of amendment to the Constitution of the United States is hereby repealed.

2: The transportation or importation into any State, Territory, or possession of the United States for delivery or use therein of intoxicating liquors, in violation of the laws thereof, is hereby prohibited.

3: This article shall be inoperative unless it shall have been ratified as an amendment to the Constitution by conventions in the several States, as provided in the Constitution, within seven years from the date of the submission hereof to the States by the Congress.

Twenty-Second Amendment

1: NO PERSON SHALL be elected to the office of the President more than twice, and no person who has held the office of President, or acted as President, for more than two years of a term to which some other person was elected President shall be elected to the office of the President more than once. But this article shall not apply to any person holding the office of President when this article was proposed by the Congress, and shall not prevent any person who may be holding the office of President, or acting as President, during the term within which this article becomes operative from holding the office of President or acting as President during the remainder of such term.

2: This article shall be inoperative unless it shall have been ratified as an amendment to the Constitution by the legislatures of three-fourths of the several states within seven years from the date of its submission to the states by the Congress.

Twenty-Third Amendment

1: THE DISTRICT CONSTITUTING the seat of government of the United States shall appoint in such manner as the Congress may direct: A number of electors of President and Vice President equal to the whole number of Senators and Representatives in Congress to which the District would be entitled if it were a state, but in no event more than the least populous state; they shall be in addition to those appointed by the states, but they shall be considered, for the purposes of the election of President and Vice President, to be electors appointed by a state; and they shall meet in the District and perform such duties as provided by the twelfth article of amendment.

2: The Congress shall have power to enforce this article by appropriate legislation.

Twenty-Fourth Amendment

1. The right of citizens of the United States to vote in any primary or other election for President or Vice President, for electors for President or Vice President, or for Senator or Representative in Congress, shall not be denied or abridged by the United States or any state by reason of failure to pay any poll tax or other tax.
2.
3. The Congress shall have power to enforce this article by appropriate legislation.
4.

Twenty-Fifth Amendment

1: IN CASE OF THE REMOVAL of the President from office or of his death or resignation, the Vice President shall become President.

2: Whenever there is a vacancy in the office of the Vice President, the President shall nominate a Vice President who shall take office upon confirmation by a majority vote of both Houses of Congress.

3: Whenever the President transmits to the President pro tempore of the Senate and the Speaker of the House of Representatives his written declaration that he is unable to discharge the powers and duties of his office, and until he transmits to them a written declaration to the contrary, such powers and duties shall be discharged by the Vice President as Acting President.

4: Whenever the Vice President and a majority of either the principal officers of the executive departments or of such other body as Congress may by law provide, transmit to the President pro tempore of the Senate and the Speaker of the House of Representatives their written declaration that the President is unable to discharge the powers and duties of his office, the Vice President shall immediately assume the powers and duties of the office as Acting President.

Thereafter, when the President transmits to the President pro tempore of the Senate and the Speaker of the House of Representatives his written declaration that no inability exists, he shall resume the powers and duties of his office unless the Vice President and a majority of either the principal officers of the executive department or of such other body as Congress may by law provide, transmit within four days to the President pro tempore of the Senate and the Speaker of the House of Representatives their written declaration that the President is unable to discharge the powers and duties of his office. Thereupon Congress shall decide the issue, assembling within forty-eight hours for that purpose if not in session. If the Congress, within twenty-one days after receipt of the latter written declaration, or, if Congress is not in session, within twenty-one days after Congress is required to assemble, determines by two-thirds vote of both Houses that the President is unable to discharge the powers and duties of his office, the Vice President shall continue to discharge the same as Acting President; otherwise, the President shall resume the powers and duties of his office.

Twenty-Sixth Amendment

1: THE RIGHT OF CITIZENS of the United States, who are 18 years of age or older, to vote, shall not be denied or abridged by the United States or any state on account of age.

2: The Congress shall have the power to enforce this article by appropriate legislation.

Twenty-Seventh Amendment

NO LAW VARYING THE compensation for the services of the Senators and Representatives shall take effect until an election of Representatives shall have intervened.

WE THE PEOPLE: IT BEGINS WITH YOU!

That's the Constitution and it's amendments. I recommend to everyone that wants to be informed of your Constitutional rights here in America to read and get to know it. I think maybe some of us having taken these rights for granted and at some level don't know they continue to exist. In the resource page at the back of the book I included some links to some great websites to learn more.

References

_____Constitution Annotated[1]

HTTPS://CONSTITUTION.congress.gov/constitution/[2]

"US Constitution." Cong. Rsch. Serv., Constitution of the United States: Analysis and Interpretation, https://constitution.congress.gov (last visited September 27, 2022)[3]

_____Total History[4]

HTTPS://TOTALLYHISTORY.com/united-states-constitution/ Download PDF version of constitution[5]

https://constitutionus.com/books/us_constitution_pdf/[6]

Resources

Community resources
https://www.hud.gov/i_want_to/
get_involved_in_my_community[1]
Elected Officials
https://www.usa.gov/elected-officials/[2]
Directory of Representatives
https://www.house.gov/representatives[3]
Senators
https://www.senate.gov/senators/[4]
Kids
http://kidgovernor.org/student-action-resource-center/writing-to-your-elected-officials
School Systems
https://nces.ed.gov/ccd/districtsearch/
Volunteer
https://www.volunteermatch.org/[5] https://www.habitat.org/about[6]
Self-Care Help
Mindfulness 101 course
https://illuminate-u.teachable.com/p/mindfulness-101

---

1. http://www.hud.gov/i_want_to/get_involved_in_my_community

2. http://www.usa.gov/elected-officials/

3. http://www.house.gov/representatives

4. http://www.senate.gov/senators/

5. http://www.volunteermatch.org/

6. http://www.habitat.org/about

Self-Care Course (Coming Soon)
https://illuminate-u.teachable.com
Self-Care Products https://kellysherbalblessings.com/shop/
Blog
https://www.illuminatingselfgrowth.com/[7]
Follow us on Facebook
https://www.facebook.com/IlluminatingSelfGrowth[8]

---

7.   http://www.illuminatingselfgrowth.com/

8.   http://www.facebook.com/IlluminatingSelfGrowth

About the Author

KELLY MOYER WAS BORN and raised in Canton, Ohio, and has spent her life walking many paths—with each one adding depth to her purpose and passion. From a successful career in data and technology to a deep journey into healing and self-growth, Kelly's life is a testament to transformation, resilience, and service.

As a certified Reiki Master and energy healer, Kelly is deeply committed to helping others rediscover their inner light. She believes in the power of personal responsibility and the beauty of consciously creating a peaceful, purposeful life. Through her platform, *Illuminating Self-Growth*, she offers courses like *Mindfulness 101* to guide others toward clarity, calm, and connection.

In 2021, Kelly expanded her passion for natural wellness by founding *Kelly's Herbal Blessings*, a self-care brand rooted in herbal healing, relaxation, and raising positive energy. What began as a labor of love—making holistic products for family and friends—has grown into a thriving business sharing handcrafted, clean self-care products with the world.

Kelly envisions a world where compassion, unity, and love rise above chaos and division. She believes in uplifting one another, embracing the beauty in everyday life, and nurturing the earth and each other for future generations.

Now living in Southern California, Kelly finds joy in the simple things—morning coffee in the garden, barefoot walks along the beach, and time spent with her three grown children and grandchildren. Whether through her writing, courses, or herbal offerings, she continues to be a light for those seeking healing, hope, and a more meaningful life.

You can connect with Kelly at www.illuminatingselfgrowth.com1 or explore her handcrafted wellness products at www.kellysherbalblessings.com.

Don't miss out!

Visit the website below and you can sign up to receive emails whenever Kelly Moyer publishes a new book. There's no charge and no obligation.

https://books2read.com/r/B-A-VFRFE-ZNFRG

BOOKS 2 READ

Connecting independent readers to independent writers.

www.ingramcontent.com/pod-product-compliance
Lightning Source LLC
LaVergne TN
LVHW041205080426
835508LV00008B/812